Language Development for Science

Activities for Home

Marion Nash and Jackie Lowe

 David Fulton Publishers

David Fulton Publishers Ltd
The Chiswick Centre, 414 Chiswick High Road, London W4 5TF

David Fulton Publishers is a division of Granada Learning Limited, part of ITV plc.

10 9 8 7 6 5 4 3 2 1

First published in Great Britain by David Fulton Publishers 2005.

www.fultonpublishers.co.uk

Illustrations by Phillipa Drakeford.

British Library Cataloguing in Publication Data
A catalogue record for this book is available from the British Library.

ISBN: 1-84312-174-3

Typeset by FiSH Books, London
Printed and bound in Great Britain

Contents

Appendices

Background

This book has been written to accompany *Language Development for Science: Circle Time Sessions to Improve Language Skills* (see pages 67–8 for details). It is one of a series of books which support the Spirals programme of language development. This programme has been trialled in a number of schools and is proving highly successful in improving children's language skills, confidence and self-esteem.

Parents often express a wish to help their children with activities at home, which are effective but also achievable in a busy lifestyle. These simple, play-based activities will help busy parents, carers and support workers to focus on the language that is used at home to aid the development of their children's learning in science.

We have taken one key idea from each weekly Spirals session and built up a bank of learning experiences. These activity sheets can be photocopied and given to parents and carers to empower them to work in collaboration with their children's setting. The handbook can also stand alone in providing ideas for parents, teachers and speech and language therapists.

Jackie Lowe and Marion Nash

Acknowledgements

The publication of this book has been made possible by the enthusiasm, foresight and support of those people working in the Plymouth Teaching Primary Care Trust and the Plymouth Education Authority. We have been supported and encouraged by the managers and those who direct these services.

We must also acknowledge and thank those parents and professionals who worked with us, in developing the Spirals approach to the language of science, within the Plymouth area.

Using the handbook

The ideas in this book are linked directly to the 36 sessions in the book *Language Development for Science: Circle Time Sessions* to improve language skills, which underpins the Spirals course (see pages 67–8).

Each page is designed to be used as a stand-alone handout to develop one key idea in a simple and user-friendly way. Parents and carers can use the ideas as play activities with their children at home.

The illustrations may also be given to act as a prompt for parents whose literacy skills are weak, or for whom English is an additional language. Coloured in and pinned to a wall at home, they also act as a visual reminder of simple games that can continue to be fun for all members of the family.

The aim is that one sheet will be given out after each session to reinforce concepts which have been introduced in that session. Active use of these sheets at home will further accelerate the children's learning and understanding, and encourage parents' involvement in establishing a strong bedrock for learning. Using these sheets will empower parents to work in collaboration with their child's setting and give them confidence that they are 'doing the right thing'.

The grid on each page is for the parent to indicate how the activity went – did it go very well, with the child enjoying it and showing by the end that he or she had understood the word and concept? The empty boxes are for the parent to tick and/or date each time they try the activity. If the sheets are handed in after use, this device can help the teacher to understand how much support is being offered at home; it can also act as a motivator for parents and carers.

Date	☺ Comment

Date	☺ Comment
4/5/04	Jason likes this
5/5/04	game. His sister
7/5/04	joined in. ☺

The worksheets in this book may also be used independently where necessary, to give support in particular areas of language development.

The record sheets at the end of the book may be used by parents and/or teachers to keep track of activities used.

Ideas
for
Home

Smell

Ideas for Home

Play the smelling game

Session 1: Understanding and using the sense of smell, associating the word <u>smell</u>

Date:...........

Ask your child to show you their nose. Say, 'Where is your nose?'. Say, 'That's right, that is your nose and this is my nose. We use our noses to smell things.'

Find a mixture of items from around the house that smell (e.g. soap, coffee, chocolate). Smell these with your child and talk about things that smell. Do they smell nice?

Find a mixture of items from around the house that don't smell (e.g. a plate, a glass, a cup). Try and smell them and explore together that they have no smell.

During the week encourage your child to use their sense of smell as much as they can. Talk about smells and explore things that smell and things that don't smell. Talk about using your nose to smell.

Date	☺ Comment

Touch

Ideas for Home

Play the feely game

Session 2: Understanding and using the sense of <u>touch</u>, associating the word <u>smooth</u>

Date:...........

Ask your child to show you their fingers. Rub your fingertips lightly together and say, 'We use our fingers to feel things and to touch.' Encourage your child to do this with you.

Say, 'We are going to play a touchy feely game together'.

Find a tea towel and, without your child seeing, put something underneath it (e.g. a fork).

Without looking, put your hand under the cloth and say, 'I can feel some things. What can this be? It feels cold and smooth and hard. What can it be?'

Don't allow your child to look but encourage them to feel. Talk to them about what they feel underneath the cloth.

Ask them, 'Is it smooth, cold, hard?'

Then see if they can guess what it might be. 'Do you know what it is?'

Play the game again hiding a different object (e.g. a magazine) and see if they can tell you what it feels like. It is very important that your child doesn't see the object first, and don't allow them to just guess what it is! Encourage them to use the words that they can feel (e.g. smooth, hard, cold or soft).

Date	☺ Comment

Looking and seeing

Ideas for Home

Play the looking game

Session 3: Understanding and using the sense of sight, associating the words <u>look</u> and <u>sight</u> with eyes

Date:............

Ask your child to show you their eyes. Say, 'Where are your eyes?', 'Where are my eyes?'. Encourage your child to look at your eyes and see what colour they are. Say to your child, 'We use eyes for looking and seeing.'

Say, 'We are going to play some games without using our eyes'.

Make a space in a room at home with you sitting with your child, and someone else sitting on the other side of the room but with no obstacles in between. Ask your child to walk to the other person. Then ask the other person to put a blindfold on your child and talk to them about how they can't see. The other person turns them around and says, 'Now let's walk back', takes their hand and walks across the room. Give your child lots of praise for doing this. Give them a cuddle, then see if they can walk back alone to the other person, with the blindfold on.

Talk to your child about how we use our eyes to see, and how this helps to tell us where we are and who people are and what things are.

Play blindfold games together in the week to encourage your child to understand the value of sight.

Date	☺ Comment

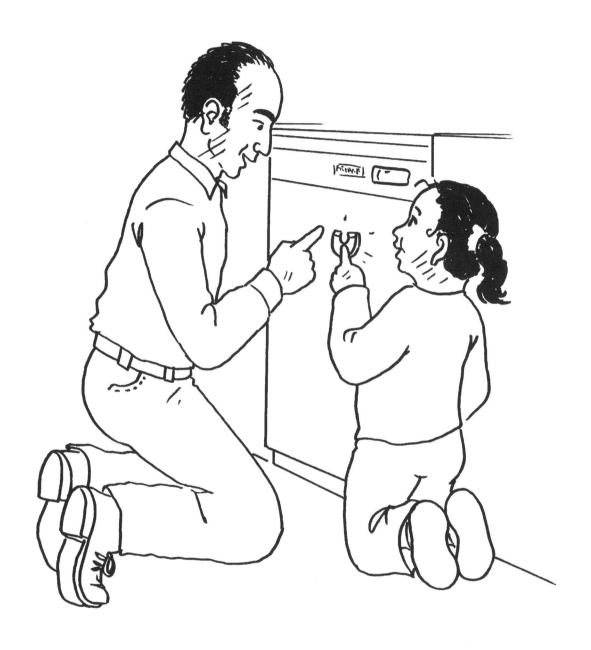

Magnets

Ideas for Home

Play with magnets

Session 4: Understanding and using magnets, and using the word <u>magnet</u> (you will need a fridge magnet)

Date:............

With your child take the fridge magnet and explore the metal bit at the back. Tell your child, 'This is called a magnet. It sticks to some things.'

Show your child how the fridge magnet sticks to the fridge. Let them feel how it works and explore the pull of the magnet.

Explore with your child some of the objects it sticks to around your house and some of the objects it doesn't stick to. Try it on something wooden (e.g. a door or a wooden spoon), try it on the bath and the taps, try it on the sofa, the washing machine and on a spoon.

Make a collection of items the magnet sticks to and doesn't stick to.

Try and use the word 'magnet' as much as you can during the week.

Date	☺ Comment

Ideas for Home

Play the feely game again

Session 5: Understanding and using the word <u>rough</u>, and using the sense of touch to find out

Date:............

You will need to have thought about where some rough textures are in your house or garden. Examples might be a breeze-block wall or a piece of wood or bark of a tree.

Ask your child to show you their fingers. Rub your fingertips lightly together and say, 'We use our fingers to feel things and to touch.' Encourage your child to do this with you.

Say, 'We are going to play a touchy feely game together again today.

Walk around the house and garden with your child touching and feeling surfaces, and say, 'This table feels smooth.'

Take your child to a surface that feels rough and say, 'This... feels different, this feels rough.' Try and find at least three objects around your home and garden that feel rough to the touch and each time say, 'This feels rough to touch.'

During the week try to encourage your child to use their sense of touch to decide if things feel smooth or rough. Sometimes things will feel a bit of each or you may not be sure what they feel like. Discuss this with your child.

Date	☺ Comment

Ideas for Home

Play the listening game

Session 6: Understanding and using the word <u>hear</u>, and using the sense of hearing to find out

Date:............

Ask your child to show you their ears. Say, 'Where are your ears?'. Say, 'That's right. These are your ears and these are my ears. We use our ears to hear with.'

Prepare some sound makers from objects within the home (e.g. a spoon in a mug, a spoon in a tin, a spoon in an empty cereal box, some water in a bottle).

Show your child what you have made and then make a sound with each one. Encourage them to make sounds with them as well. Encourage your child to close their eyes, or put the objects behind a screen or cloth and make one sound and see if they can identify which sound they can hear.

Give them lots of praise and say you can hear that sound and that was very clever. Then place the different sound makers around the room. Say, 'We are going to play a hearing game. You have to use your ears to hear. I am going to ask you to tell me where a sound is coming from.' With your child's eyes closed see if they can tell you by pointing where you are making a sound.

Ideas for earlier games to do with listening may be found in *Language Development: Activities for Home* (ISBN 1-84312-170-0), pages 2 and 17.

Date	☺ Comment

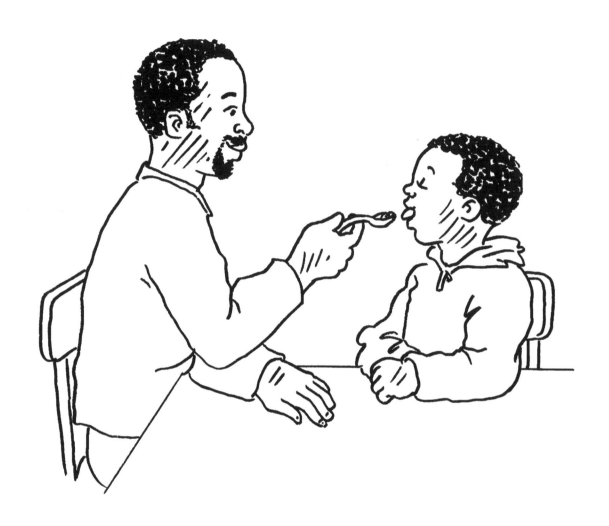

Tasting

Ideas for Home

Play the tasting game

Session 7: Understanding and using the words <u>mouth</u>, <u>tongue</u> and <u>taste</u>, and understanding the sense of taste

Date:............

You will need some foods that have different tastes, e.g. sweet (sweets or chocolate), sour (lemon) or salty (crisps).

Ask your child to show you their mouth. Say, 'Where is your mouth?'. Say, 'That's right! That is your mouth, and this is my mouth.' Then ask your child to show you his tongue.

Say, 'We use our mouths and tongues to taste things.'

Prepare some foods for your child to taste. Eat them together and talk together about what they taste like. Use the words 'sweet,' 'sour-bitter', 'salty'.

During the week encourage your child to use their sense of taste and say whether things taste sweet or sour or salty.

Date	☺ Comment

Day and night

Ideas for Home

Talk about day and night

Session 8: Using the words <u>day</u> and <u>night</u>

Date:............

When it is light outside look out of the window together at the sky and say, 'It is light outside and you can see things. When it is light outside it is daytime. In the day we play with our friends and go shopping and visit people.'

When it is dark outside look out of the window with your child and say, 'It is dark outside. I can see the moon and the stars [point these out to your child] and you can't see things easily. This is called night-time. When it is night-time we usually go to bed and sleep.'

During the week talk to your child as much as you can about day and night and light and dark.

Ideas for earlier games involving teaching day and night may be found in *Language Development for Maths: Activities for Home* (ISBN 1-84312-172-7), pages 47 and 49.

Date	☺ Comment

Ideas for Home

Talk about dark and light

Session 9: Understanding the words <u>dark</u> and <u>light</u> and how we need light to see

Date:............

One day in the evening when it is dark outside look outside at the sky and say, 'It is dark. We must put the light on.' When you put the light on say, 'It is light now.'

Help your child to notice that putting a light on makes light when it is dark.

When it is light outside say to your child, 'I am going to put the light on.' Then encourage your child to think about whether you need the light on to see.

Pull the curtains so that it is dark and ask your child if they can see. Encourage them to say, 'Put on the light.'

Talk about this during the week.

- Look in a dark cupboard together and talk about needing the light on to see.
- Look in a dark drawer together and talk about needing a light or torch to see.

Encourage your child to use the words 'light' and 'dark' as much as possible during the week.

Date	☺ Comment

Ideas for Home

Play another smelling game

Session 10: Understanding and using the sense of smell, associating the word <u>smell</u> and using smell without sight

Date:............

You will need to collect some items from around the house that have different smells (e.g. soap, chocolate, coffee, cut apple or orange).

Say to your child, 'We are going to play a guessing game with smells.' You can play this game with other family members as well.

Make a collection of things that smell and then blindfold one of the players. While they are blindfolded another member has to choose one of the smelling objects and place it gently, so they can't feel it, under the blindfolded person's nose. The idea is that the blindfolded person has to smell and guess the item. If they guess correctly they can take the blindfold off and another person has a go.

When your child guesses correctly give them lots of praise for 'good detective smelling'.

Date	☺ Comment

Light

Ideas for Home

Play with light

Session 11: Understanding and playing with <u>light</u>

Date:..........

You will need a small torch for this activity.

Show your child the torch and how it can be turned on and off. Talk about how, when it is turned on, it gives light.

Get your child's duvet or a blanket and go beneath it with your child with the torch switched off. Tuck yourself well under so that it is dark. Look at your child and say, 'We have made it all dark under here, we can't see very well.' Then turn on the torch and talk about how now you can see because you have light from the torch.

Ask your child to climb out from under the duvet while you stay underneath with the torch on. Ask your child, 'Can you see the torch light?'

Talk about the light shining through.

Spend some more time with the torch, using it to light up areas that are dark such as under the carpet and the bed.

Date	☺ Comment

Ideas for Home

Play with light some more

Session 12: Understanding that light passes through some materials but not others

Date:............

You will need a small torch for this activity.

Talk about the torch and how it can light up dark places. Collect a mixture of different materials (e.g. a piece of clingfilm, a piece of toilet paper, a book, a cereal box).

Turn on the torch and ask your child to go to the other side of the door and shut it. Ask your child if they can see the light from the torch shining through the wood.

Work with your child to find out what materials the light shines through and what it doesn't shine through. Does it shine through glass, clingfilm, wood, a book? Make a collection.

Say to your child, 'Some materials are transparent and light can pass through them, and some are not and light can't pass through.'

Continue to look at materials and try to decide whether light will pass through them or not.

Date	☺ Comment

Ideas for Home

Talk about the word 'hot'

Session 13: Understanding the different uses of the word <u>hot</u> and what we can do to change our body temperature

Date:...........

Talk to your child about the word 'hot'. Make a hot drink for yourself and say, 'This is a hot drink.' Encourage your child to feel the heat through the mug.

Say to your child that you like a hot drink when you are cold to warm yourself up. During the week talk about how you feel hot when you are in the sun or walking. If you have the opportunity when you are hot, say to your child, 'I am hot.' If your child is hot after running, say, 'You are hot now.' When your child is hot say, 'In order to cool down you must take your jumper off or sit down and have a rest.'

During the week talk about being hot and then talk about what you do to cool yourself down. Sit down, have a cold drink, take some clothes off, use a newspaper as a fan. When you eat a hot meal talk about it being a hot meal and say, 'This is a hot meal. It has been heated up in the oven.'

Date	☺ Comment

Cold

Ideas for Home

Talk about the word 'cold'

Session 14: Understanding the different meanings of the word cold and what we can do to change our body temperature

Date:............

Talk to your child about the word 'cold'. Make a cold drink for yourself and say, 'This is a cold drink.' Encourage your child to feel the cold through the glass. Say to your child that you like a cold drink when you are hot to cool yourself down.

Talk about what makes you feel cold, when it is windy or snowy in the winter or when there is no heating. Say to your child, 'I am cold because....' If your child is cold, say, 'You are cold.' When your child is cold, say, 'In order to warm up you must put some more clothes on and go somewhere warm, put the fire on, jump up and down or have a hot drink.'

During the week talk about being cold and then talk about what you do to warm yourself up. Wear more clothes, gloves and scarves, switch on the heating or light the fire or eat or drink something hot.

Date	☺ Comment

Shadows

Ideas for Home

Making shadows

Session 15: Understanding the word <u>shadow</u>

Date:............

You will need a small torch.

Turn the torch on and shine it on to your hand so that your hand makes a shadow on the wall. Move your fingers around so that they dance and then say to your child, 'I have made a shadow.' Encourage your child to do the same and name it as a shadow.

Make shapes with the shadow and encourage your child to make shadows of other objects (e.g. a book or a flower).

Encourage your child to look around when you have a normal light on and see if they can see a shadow.

Look outside when the sun is shining to see if they can find shadows.

Talk about how some shadows stay still (e.g. a tree, a lamp-post) and how some shadows move (e.g. people, dogs).

Date	☺ Comment

Ideas for Home

Play the senses game

Session 16: Making a choice about different <u>senses</u> that may be used

Date:...........

You will need to collect some objects together (e.g. an apple, a spoon, a cup, a segment of orange, a bar of soap, a comic).

This is a game you can play alone with your child or in a family group.

Say to your child, 'We are going to play a guessing game but this time you can choose which sense you use to guess. So you can use your touchy fingers, or your smell.'

If your child chooses touchy feeling fingers, place the object under a cloth for them to feel. If they choose smell, the person needs to be blindfolded before being given the object.

Talk about which things were easier to guess and which were harder.

Date	☺ Comment

Ideas for Home

Exploring living things

Session 17: Exploring what things are <u>living</u> and what are <u>not living</u>

Date:............

You will need to think about what are living things in and around your home. If you haven't got any pets of your own try and think of some pets that are familiar to your child. Also look around at what trees and plants are near you.

Sit down with your child when they are having a drink and some food and say to them, 'You need food and drink and air to breathe to stay alive. I need food and drink and air to breathe to stay alive too. You and me and...[mention other family members] are all living, and we need food and drink and air to stay alive.'

Ask your child if they know of anything else that is living.

Encourage them to tell you about their pets or a friend or neighbour's pets. Spend time talking to them about what the pets eat and drink, and how they breathe and sleep and move. Talk about dogs, cats, fish.

Take your child for a walk. Look at the grass, plants and trees. Say to your child, 'These are living too. They don't walk or sleep but they need food and drink and light to stay alive and grow.'

Talk about living things as much as possible during the week.

Date	☺ Comment

27

Living things

Ideas for Home

Play the 'spot hunt for living things' game

Session 18: Exploring things that are <u>living</u> and what they need to stay <u>alive</u>

Date:............

Think of a little walk near you where your child can see a tree, some grass and some plants.

Take your child's hand and say, 'We are going to look for some living things.'

As you walk with your child say, 'I have seen something living' and see if they can guess what it is. If they do guess, give them lots of praise and talk about what it drinks and eats. For example, 'It has roots under the ground that soak up the water and food from out of the soil.'

If they can't guess, show them the object, name it and talk about how it gets its food and drink. Say again, 'I can see something else living' and see if they can guess what it is. Play this game until they have found a tree, a plant and some grass as well as other animals (e.g. birds, butterflies, insects). See if you can remember all the living things you found on your walk.

Play the 'spot hunt for living things' walk again in the week until your child is confident with talking about living things.

Date	☺ Comment

Roots

Ideas for Home

Look at roots together

Session 19: Exploringing <u>roots</u> and how they work

Date:.............

You will need to pull up some grass with its roots on or take a small plant out of its pot. Show your child the roots of the grass or plant and let them touch and feel the roots. Say, 'The grass uses the roots to get water and food from the soil. If it can't do this, it will die.'

Talk about leaves and stems as well.

During the week talk about roots as much as you can and how plants and trees need them.

Play a game, asking your child some silly questions (e.g. 'Is a chair living?', 'Is a tree living?', 'Is a table living?') to help your child be able to decide if something is living or not.

Date	☺ Comment

Push and pull

Ideas for Home

Playing the 'pulling and pushing' game

Session 20: Using the words <u>push</u> and <u>pull</u>, and associating them with the word <u>force</u>

Date:............

You will need a kitchen roll cardboard inner tube and a tea-towel or carrier bag from the supermarket.

Show your child the cardboard tube and say, 'I am going to push the towel through the tube. Watch as I'm pushing.' As the tube gets stiff say, 'I need to be very strong now and use lots of force to push the towel through.' Then show your child the other end and say, 'Now I am going to pull the towel out of the end.'

Encourage your child to have a go at playing the pulling and pushing game and to say what he is doing – pushing or pulling. As it gets tight say, 'You are using lots of force now, well done!'

During the week talk to your child about being strong and how some things need force to work (e.g. opening a new jam jar lid or pushing something heavy).

Date	☺ Comment

Different clothes

Ideas for Home

Play the 'sorting clothes' game

Session 21: Learning about clothes and why we wear them, to keep us warm or cool

Date:...........

Collect some of your child's clothes (some summer clothes and some winter clothes) (e.g. a T-shirt, a scarf, a coat, some shorts, gloves).

Look at the clothes together and say, 'These are some of your clothes. Some of them you wear when it is hot and some of them you wear when it is cold. Which ones do you wear when it is cold?' Encourage your child to put in a pile the clothes they would wear when it is cold. Say, 'Yes, this would warm you up.'

Ask your child to find clothes they would wear when they were hot, and encourage them to put these in a pile. Say, 'Yes, you would wear this if it was hot and you wanted to stay cool.'

During the week when your child is getting dressed and putting on or taking off their clothes, talk about whether that will make them warm or keep them cool.

Date	☺ Comment

Fur

Ideas for Home

Think about pets

Session 22: Looking at pets and talking about <u>fur</u>, and how animals keep warm or cool

Date:............

You will need to think of where you can find a friendly cat/dog/rabbit.

Take your child's hand and gently stroke its fur together. Say, 'This is fur. How does it feel? Does it feel soft or prickly or smooth?' Encourage your child to feel and say what they can feel.

Fur helps to keep the pet warm.

Ask, 'Does it wear clothes?' 'What does it do if it gets too hot or too cold?'

Encourage your child to think, and then say it sits by the fire to get warm, it has a drink, or it lies down on a cool floor to cool down.

Date	☺ Comment

Feathers

Ideas for Home

Think about birds

Date:............

You will need to find a feather and think about where you might see a bird.

Look at the feather together and say, 'This is a feather. Birds have feathers on their bodies.'

Take your child's hand and go for a walk and see if you can find a bird. When you have spotted a bird say to your child, 'There is a bird. A bird has feathers and flies in the sky.' Spend some time watching the birds and how they fly. See if one will come near you.

Talk about what a bird eats and drinks, and how it keeps warm.

Date	☺ Comment

Movement

Ideas for Home

Play the 'animal moving' game

Session 24: Talking and thinking about how different animals move

Date:............

Say to your child, 'We are going to play a guessing game. I am going to move and you have to tell me what animal I am pretending to be.'

Then you pretend to fly and see if your child can guess it's a bird.

If they can't, help them and try another animal (e.g. a dog, cat, person, rabbit).

Encourage your child to have a go at being an animal and see if you can guess which animal they are.

Play this game again during the week and use the words 'walk', 'fly', 'hop', 'slither'.

Date	☺ Comment

Ideas for Home

Play the 'sugar dissolving' game

Session 25: Understanding the word <u>dissolve</u>

Date:...........

You will need a spoonful of sugar, a cup and a spoon.

Fetch a cupful of water. Say to your child, 'Taste this!' and give them a taste of the water. Say, 'This is water.'

Then say to your child, 'Look at this!' and show them a spoonful of sugar. 'I'm going to put it into the water. Watch.' Then put the sugar into a cup of water. Say, 'Look!' and use the spoon to bring up the sugar so you can see the grains. Say, 'There are the grains of sugar in the water.' Then stir the water very quickly. Continue to stop every so often and bring up the spoon to see if the grains can still be seen. Slowly the grains will get smaller and smaller until they have gone. Then say to your child, 'The grains have gone...they have dissolved in the water.' Then allow your child to sip the water and taste the sweetness. Say, 'See, the sugar has dissolved into the water and the water now tastes sweet!'

Talk about what else might dissolve in water. Talk about how when the water is hot, things dissolve more quickly (e.g. in coffee).

Date	☺ Comment

Ideas for Home

What dissolves and what doesn't

Session 26: Exploring what <u>dissolves</u> and what doesn't

Date:...........

You will need a cupful of water and a mixture of things that dissolve and things that don't (e.g. slice of apple, a pencil, a paper-clip, some salt, a piece of chocolate).

Say, 'We are going to play a guessing game – do you think this will dissolve in the water or not?' Hold up the paper-clip and ask, 'Will this dissolve in the water?' See what your child says. Then put the paper-clip into the water and stir it with the spoon, and watch to see if it dissolves. When it doesn't, say, 'No, it doesn't dissolve', then place it to one side. Go through all the things you have collected and you will be left with a pile of things that don't dissolve. Say, 'These don't dissolve. Can we remember the things that do dissolve – like sugar and salt?'

Talk about things that disappear when they dissolve and things that change the colour of the water (e.g. soil).

Date	☺ Comment

43

Reflections

Ideas for Home

Play the 'reflection' game

Session 27: Understanding the word <u>reflection</u>

Date:............

You will need to think of a walk where your child will have the chance to see reflections (e.g. in a large shop window or glass door).

Take your child's hand and say, 'We're going to look for reflections.' When you have the opportunity to see yourselves in a large shop window or glass door say, 'There is your reflection!' Make sure your child has the chance to see a reflection at least three times on the walk.

When you get home talk about reflections and see if you can see reflections in other things (e.g. the screen of a television when it is switched off, your windows when it is dark outside, the glass of a framed picture).

Date	☺ Comment

Reflections in the mirror

Ideas for Home

More 'reflection' games

Session 28: Talking about <u>reflections in the mirror</u>

Date:............

You will need a mirror.

Look in the mirror with your child and show interest in all that you see. Say, 'That is a reflection of you!' Spend time asking your child to show you:

'What do we smell with?'
'What do we hear with?'
'What do we taste with?'
'What do we see with?'

If your child finds this difficult, help them, and reinforce with, 'We smell with our noses', 'We hear with our ears.'

If they find this easy give them lots of praise for remembering.

Date	☺ Comment

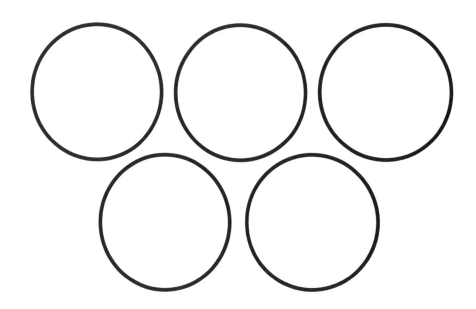

Patterns

Ideas for Home

Explore patterns

Session 29: Understanding the word <u>pattern</u>

Date:...........

You will need some paper and a pencil.

Say to your child, 'Watch me.'

Then draw a zigzag line and say, 'That's a zigzag line.' Add to it some dots at the top. Then say, 'Look! I have made a pattern.' (A pattern is a repeated sequence.) 'I'm going to make more of a pattern. I can draw a circle but if I draw lots in the same place I have drawn a pattern!'

Spend some time drawing lots of different patterns. Use different colours.

Ask your child which one he likes best.

See if your child can draw a pattern.

Emphasise the word 'pattern'.

Date	☺ Comment

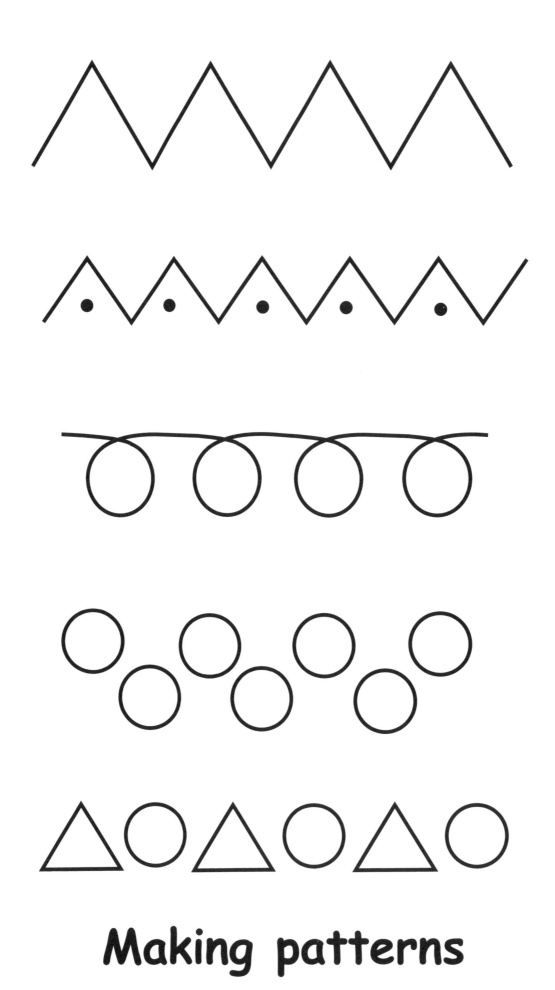

Making patterns

Ideas for Home

Make more patterns

Session 30: Making <u>patterns</u> together

Date:............

You will need to draw some shapes (e.g. circles, squares, stars and triangles all the same size) or use the photocopiable material provided at the back of this book.

Cut out the shapes with your child and say, 'We can make some patterns with these.' Start to make some patterns and then encourage your child to make some patterns as well. Talk about the patterns and which ones you like best.

Later in the week colour the patterned shapes and play the game again. Talk about how this makes it more difficult because there are now different colours, so it's not as easy to repeat the sequence.

Date	☺ Comment

Finding patterns

Ideas for Home

Go on a pattern hunt

Session 31: Identifying patterns in the house

Date:............

You will need to think of some objects in your house that have patterns (e.g. wallpaper, bed covers, cushions, curtains).

Take your child's hand and say, 'We are going to look for patterns. Look carefully and see if you can find any'. When you find a pattern take your child's hand and point out the pattern. Look carefully and say, 'Look! Can you see the pattern here?'

When you have spent some time looking at that pattern, move on to another pattern. Do the same thing, take your child's hand and point out the pattern together. You can find patterns on cups and tins as well. See if you can count how many patterns you find. See if you and your child together can remember where you found the patterns around your home. Say, 'Can you remember the pattern on the carpet upstairs? Can you remember the pattern on teddy's jumper?'

Date	☺ Comment

Ideas for Home

Mixing colours

Session 32: Exploring mixing <u>colours</u>

Date:............

You will need some pieces of transparent coloured paper. Your school may be able to lend these to you. Choose blue, yellow and red as first choice. (Some sweets have this type of wrapping.)

Take the coloured paper, which may be easier to handle if it is cut into small sheets. Say, 'This paper is see-through.'

Look through the paper at your child. This can be quite fun because your face will change colour. Try all the different colours and then encourage your child to ask for the coloured paper they would like to look through.

Encourage your child to name all the colours and to look through the colours at faces and his hand. Say, 'Look! Your skin has changed colour under the paper!'

Lay all the pieces down on the table. Say, 'Look at this!' and overlay the yellow on the blue to make green. Say, 'Look! It has changed colour, we have made green.' Encourage your child to overlay the colours to make different colours.

Play games overlaying all the different colours on your skin as well.

Date	☺ Comment

Ideas for Home

Using predictions

Session 33: Answering a question from a <u>prediction</u>

Date:............

Science learning requires your child to begin to answer some difficult questions in a form they may not be used to. This session is to help your child develop some of these skills.

You will need your hand torch again and a blanket.

Take the torch and switch it on and then off. Sit under the blanket with your child. Say, 'It is dark under here. If I turn the torch on what will happen next?' Encourage your child to predict that there will be light, and you will be able to see. Say, 'If I turn the torch off, what will happen next?' Encourage your child to say, 'It will be dark, we won't be able to see.'

Use questions that require your child to predict what will happen next as much as possible during the week. When reading a story, ask questions like, 'What will happen next?'

When you are getting ready to go outside and are putting your child's coat on, say, 'What will happen next?'

Date	☺ Comment

Ideas for Home

Using observations

Session 34: Answering a question from <u>observations</u>

Date:............

Science learning requires your child to begin to answer some difficult questions in a form they may not be used to. This session is to help your child develop some of these skills.

Say to your child, 'You know we talked about night and day? How do we know when it is night?' Encourage your child to answer the question by saying, 'When it's dark outside', 'When the stars are out', 'When we go to bed', or 'When ... comes home.' If they just say, 'Bed' or, 'Go to sleep' or 'No', repeat the question and then encourage them by talking about 'How we know it's night'.

Then ask your child, 'How do we know it's daytime?' Encourage your child to answer the question (e.g. 'The sun is out', 'It is light outside', '... comes to play').

Ask as many 'How do we know?' questions as you can during the week (e.g. 'How do we know this is hot?', 'How do we know he is sad?').

Date	☺ Comment

Ideas for Home

Another point of view

Session 35: Answering a question from another person's <u>point of view</u>

Date:...........

Science learning requires your child to begin to answer some difficult questions in a form they may not be used to. This session is to help your child develop some more of these skills.

Ask your child, 'If Daddy was cold, what could he do?'

Encourage your child to think and then say, 'Put on a coat', 'Sit by the fire', 'Have a hot drink'.

If they answer this well, give them lots of praise. If they say, 'Put my coat on' or 'Don't know', tell them what he could do and then ask another similar question (e.g. 'If Granny was hot, what could she do?').

Continue to ask questions during the week that encourage your child to observe from a different perspective (e.g. 'What could she do?', 'I'm hungry, what shall I do?', 'Tess is tired, what should she do?', 'Tom has lost his lunch money, what should he do?').

Date	☺ Comment

Ideas for Home

Why something can't be done

Session 36: Answering a question explaining <u>why</u> something can't be done

Date:............

Science learning requires your child to begin to answer some difficult questions in a form they may not be used to. This session is to help your child develop some more of these skills and develop some reasoning skills as well.

Think of a situation where your child can't do something because something else is happening. Perhaps you can't go to Gran's house because she is on holiday. Or you can't go shopping because the shop is shut.

Say to your child, 'We can't go to Gran's house today because she is going shopping.' Then a little while later ask your child, 'Why can't we go to Gran's today?' See if they can answer you with, 'Because she's going shopping.' If they can, give lots of praise for good listening, remembering and thinking. If they can't, encourage them by saying, 'Because she is going shopping.'

Continue to ask these sorts of questions to encourage your child to use their thinking and remembering skills.

Date	☺ Comment

Record sheet

Session 1   Play the smelling game

Session 2   Play the feely game

Session 3   Play the looking game

Session 4   Play with magnets

Session 5   Play the feely game again

Session 6   Play the listening game

Session 7   Play the tasting game

Session 8   Talk about day or night

Session 9   Talk about dark and light

Session 10   Play another smelling game

Session 11   Play with light

Session 12   Play with light some more

Record sheet

Session 13   Talk about the word 'hot'

Session 14   Talk about the word 'cold'

Session 15   Making shadows

Session 16   Play the senses game

Session 17   Explore living things

Session 18   Play the 'spot hunt for living things' game

Session 19   Look at roots together

Session 20   Play the 'pulling and pushing' game

Session 21   Play the 'sorting clothes' game

Session 22   Think about pets

Session 23   Think about birds

Session 24   Play the 'animal moving' game

Record sheet

Session 25 Play the 'sugar dissolving' game

Session 26 Explore what dissolves and what doesn't

Session 27 Play the 'reflection' game

Session 28 More 'reflection' games

Session 29 Explore patterns

Session 30 Make more patterns

Session 31 Go on a pattern hunt

Session 32 Mixing colours

Session 33 Using predictions

Session 34 Using observations

Session 35 Another point of view

Session 36 Why something can't be done

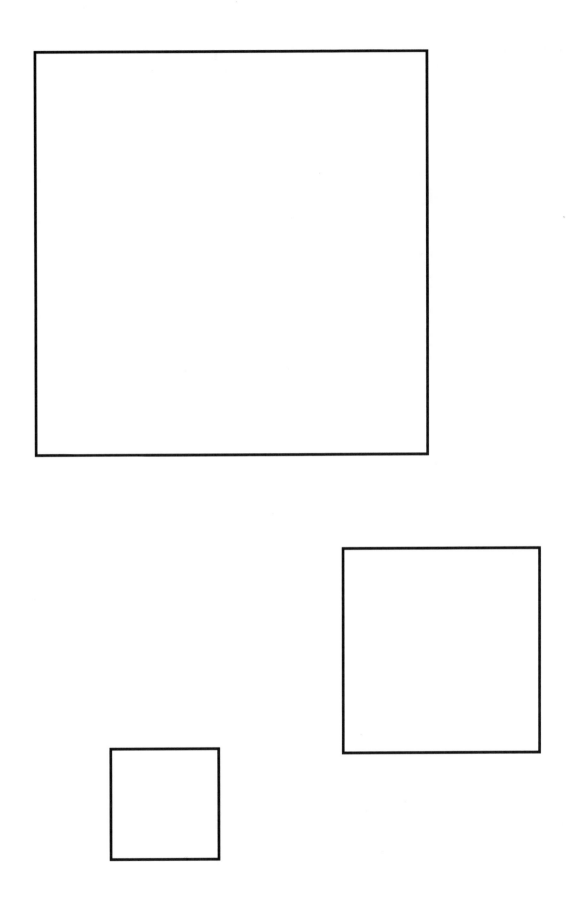

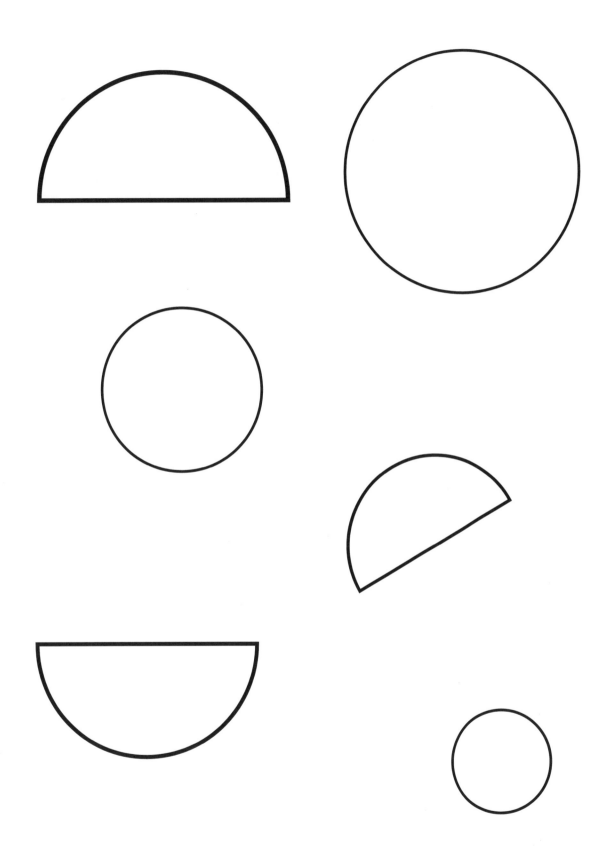

Help your children develop their language skills today!

Spirals This innovative new series addresses young children's language development needs in English, Maths and Science. Based on the spirals programme, developed by Marion Nash and successfully trialled in Plymouth schools, the books link work done in nursery or school with simple play-based activities for the children to do at home.

Ideal for Pre-school, KS1 & KS2

Focusing on English, Maths and Science the series consists of:

A class book that:

- employs a kinaesthetic approach, involving movement, singing, speaking and listening

- contains pre-planned sessions that can run over 2 terms or more

- has an accompanying Video CD providing explanations and demonstrations of the programme and its implementation, with comments from staff who have used it. Ideal for staff training!

An accompanying 'Activities for Home' book which includes:

- simple play-based activities focused on 'learning by doing' that you can photocopy and send home for parents to do with their children and reinforce the school-based sessions. The activities use everyday objects that are found at home and the book includes illustrated prompts to help parents.

> **No other books for language development focus on other core areas of the curriculum. Order yours today!**

Send your order to: David Fulton Publishers, The Chiswick Centre, 414 Chiswick High Road, London W4 5TF
Tel: 0208 996 3610 **Fax:** 0208 996 3622 **Email:** mail@fultonpublishers.co.uk **Website:** www.fultonpublishers.co.uk

English

Language Development
Circle Time Sessions
to Improve Communication
Skills
£17.00 • 144pp
1-84312-156-5 • 2003

OUT NOW!

Language Development
Activities for Home
£12.00 • 144pp
1-84312-170-0 • January 2004

Maths

Language Development for Maths
Circle Time Sessions to Improve
Language Skills
£18.00 • 144pp
1-84312-171-9 • August 2004

Aug 2004!

Language Development for Maths
Activities for Home
£12.00 • 144pp
1-84312-172-7 • August 2004

Science

Language Development for Science
Circle Time Sessions to Improve
Language Skills
£18.00 • 144pp
1-84312-173-5 • March 2005

March 2005

Language Development for Science
Activities for Home
£12.00 • 144 pp
1-84312-174-3 • March 2005

Sample activities for school

Sample activities for home

ORDER FORM

Qty	ISBN	Title	Price	Subtotal
	1-84312-156-5	Language Development	£17.00	
	1-84312-170-0	Language Development	£12.00	
	1-84312-171-9	Language Development for Maths	£18.00	
	1-84312-172-7	Language Development Maths	£12.00	
	1-84312-173-5	Language Development for Science	£18.00	
	1-84312-174-3	Language Development Science	£12.00	
			P&P	
			TOTAL	

Free p&p for Schools, LEAs and other Organisations.

Payment

☐ Please invoice
(applicable to schools, LEAs and other institutions)
Invoices will be sent from our distributor, HarperCollins Publishers

☐ I enclose a cheque payable to David Fulton Publishers Ltd
(include postage and packing)

☐ Please charge to my credit card (Visa/MasterCard, American Express, Switch, Delta)

card number ☐☐☐☐ ☐☐☐☐ ☐☐☐☐ ☐☐☐☐ ☐☐☐☐

expiry date ☐☐ ☐☐

(Switch customers only) valid from ☐☐ ☐☐   issue number ☐

Please complete delivery details

Name: ....

Organisation: ....

....

Address: ....

....

....

....

Postcode: ....

Tel: ....

To order

Send to:
David Fulton Publishers, The Chiswick Centre, 414 Chiswick High Road, London W4 5TF

Freephone:
0500 618 052

Fax:
020 8996 3622

06/04 DF315